Australian Geographic
GREAT OCEAN ROAD

By Chris Munn

WOODSLANE
PRESS

Woodslane Press Pty Ltd
10 Apollo Street
Warriewood, NSW 2102
Email: info@woodslane.com.au
Tel: 02 8445 2300 Website: www.woodslane.com.au

First published in Australia in 2019 by Woodslane Press in association with Australian Geographic
Reprinted 2024
© 2019 Woodslane Press, photographs © Australian Geographic and others
(see acknowledgements on page 62)

A catalogue record for this book is available from the National Library of Australia

NATIONAL LIBRARY OF AUSTRALIA

FSC
www.fsc.org
MIX
Supporting responsible forestry
FSC® C151165

Printed in China by Jilin GIGO
Cover image: The Twelve Apostles Cn0ra
Back cover: canbalci
Book design by: Christine Schiedel and Cory Spence

CONTENTS

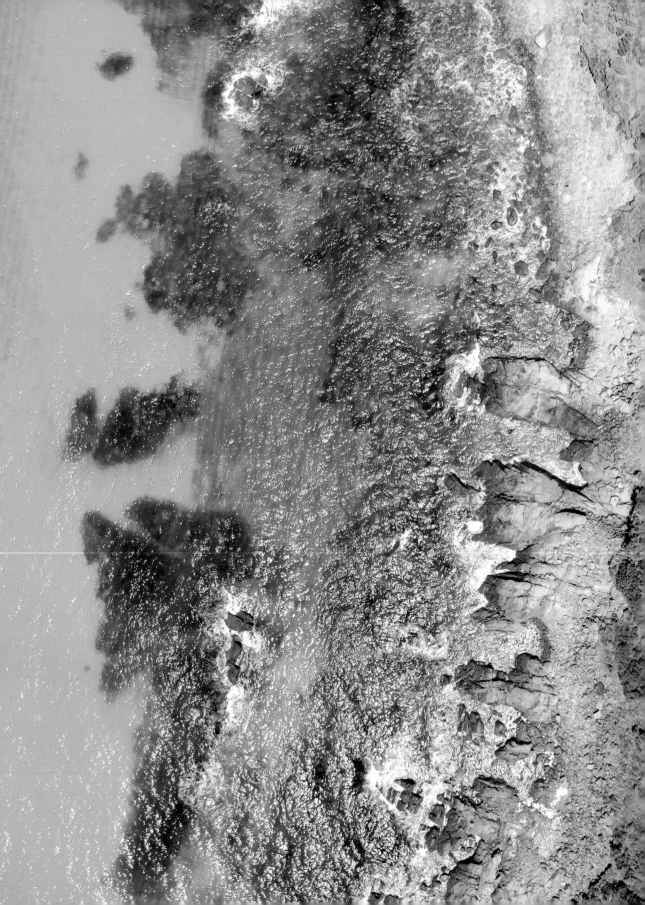

THE GREAT OCEAN ROAD

Drawing millions of visitors each year, the Great Ocean Road was born out of a vision Country Roads Board chairman William Calder had for a road to link the towns of Victoria's spectacular southwest coast. With construction beginning on 19th September 1919, as Victorian Premier Harry Lawson set off explosives near Lorne, nearly 3,000 returned servicemen worked with picks, shovels and explosives until the road was completed in 1932. Towns which once relied on access by sea or over rough bush tracks were now easily accessible by car.

At times hugging steep cliffs, frequently dividing ocean from forest, the Great Ocean Road opened up a remarkable landscape of pristine surf beaches, towering limestone headlands and a hinterland of waterfalls nestled against ancient rainforest. Recognised for its significant environmental value, much of the region is protected by marine and national parks. Wildlife is plentiful with migrating southern right whales nursing along the coast in winter, platypus drifting peacefully on Lake Elizabeth and mysterious glow worms at Melba Gully.

Visitors come to soak up romantic sunsets over the 12 Apostles, explore the rainforest and waterfalls, sample the region's produce (including cheese, chocolate, ice-cream and seafood) and spy out the wildlife. Many pass through in a day, but if you slow down and enjoy all the region has to offer you will create memories to last a lifetime

■ **Left : Cut from sea-facing cliffs with nothing more than shovels, picks and explosives, the construction of the Great Ocean Road was an engineering feat. For many returned servicemen, the use of explosives would have brought back memories of their wartime service.**

THE GREAT OCEAN ROAD

Right: The Princetown Wetlands lie within the estuary at the mouth of the Gellibrand River, which meets the Southern Ocean near the 12 Apostles, having risen in the Otway Ranges. Home to a wide array of birdlife, a boardwalk enables visitors to explore the wetlands and spot species such as the greater egret and swan.

Opposite page: Walking in some of the region's remoter spots is often the best way to find a personal connection with the landscape. Away from the crowds and alone on an isolated windswept beach, you can almost feel the remoteness of the early coastal communities. Starting at Apollo Bay and winding for 100 kilometres along the coast to Gibson Steps, the Great Ocean Walk is one of the area's premiere experiences, including breathtaking locations such as Wreck Beach.

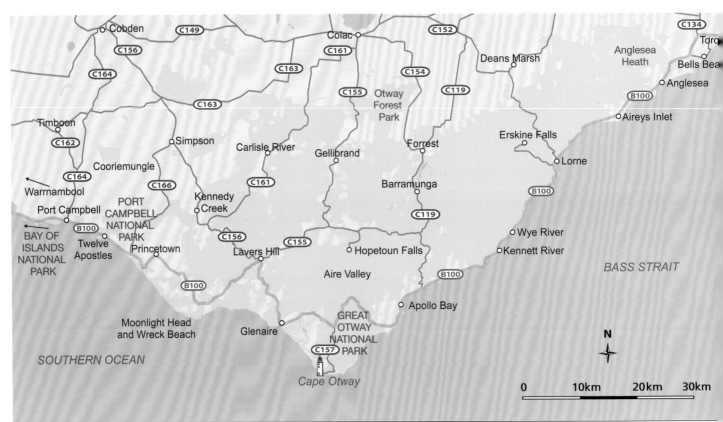

GEOLOGY

The formation of Victoria's unique south-western coastline and hinterland began aeons ago, during the Jurassic Period. At a time when dinosaurs still roamed freely across the land and warm humid conditions encouraged rainforest to flourish, the Australian land mass belonged to the ancient continent of Gondwana. As movement in the earth's tectonic plates slowly gained pace, the land masses forming Gondwana drifted apart, with Australia and Antarctica lingering as the final remnant of the ancient super continent, until they too parted ways by the Late Cretaceous period.

As the Australian continent and Antarctica drifted apart, a great rift valley opened between the two land masses, eventually being inundated by the Southern Ocean and forming the Otway Basin. Over time, marine sediment accumulated within the basin before constant folding and uplifting saw the rift valley rise out of the ocean to form the Otway Ranges and surrounding coastline. With powerful forces shaping the landscape, volcanic activity was seen at Aireys Inlet, Tower Hill and Mount Noorat. The incessant churning of the Southern Ocean against the coast has subsequently created spectacular bays, towering sea cliffs, caves and formations like the 12 Apostles.

Left: The limestone coast of Port Campbell National Park is made up of the skeletal remains of dead marine creatures that accumulated on the sea floor. Eventually the coastline rose and the ocean retreated, exposing the limestone.

Below: Tower Hill Wildlife Reserve, near Warrnambool, lies within the crater of a volcano which was formed 30,000 years ago.

CLIMATE

The Southern Ocean has a large impact on the weather patterns experienced by Victoria, as summer highs bring warm, sunny days and winter lows usher in cooler temperatures, rain and at times strong wind. Although the Great Ocean Road region can experience extremes, the climate here is relatively mild with the summer averaging 22°C maximums and winter averages in the mid-teens. Covering a wide array of geography, the conditions on any given day can vary greatly. It may be sunny at Torquay with a cool sea breeze, warm and still amongst the inland wetlands, while raining and cold deep within the Otways.

Summer is peak season, offering near perfect days for touring, exploring the 12 Apostles or swimming at one of the region's famous beaches. With cool nights, sunny days and majestic sunsets Autumn has a romantic glow and is perfect for bushwalking and camping. Spring brings variable weather and is a time when waterfalls flow and wildflowers bloom. Wet and brooding, winter is a season to feel the wild spirit of the Southern Ocean as winds whip up large swells and heavy rainfalls nourish the rainforests of the Otways.

With the right equipment and clothing, every season can be embraced and enjoyed.

SUMMER
■ (December - February)
Featuring long days with plenty of sunshine and daytime temperatures in the low to mid 20s, Summer offers the perfect weather to enjoy the region's beaches and iconic coastal formations.

AUTUMN
■ (March - May)
Autumn is a time of stable weather with cool nights and warm days where minimum and maximum temperatures range between 12-19°C along the coast. This is a great time of year, offering near perfect conditions for hiking the 'Great Ocean Walk'.

WINTER
■ (June – August),
Winter is the wettest season, with the Otway's Melba Gully recording some of the highest rainfall totals in Victoria. A time to embrace the drama of winter and explore the region's shipwreck sites and museums.

SPRING
■ (September to November)
Spring is a time of mild, unsettled weather alternating at times between gorgeous sunshine and brooding storms. Temperatures along the coast climb to an average of 18°C.

■ Right: Spring is a time of spectacular lighting along the Great Ocean Road, particularly after storms as the clouds part and the sun breaks through

ERECTED BY THE RESIDENTS & VISITORS OF PETERBOROUGH IN AFFECTIONATE MEMORY OF JAMES IRVINE WHO LOST HIS LIFE CROSSING THE RIVER 24TH JUNE 1919

Above: Shipwrecks were not the only tragedies which occurred along the Shipwreck Coast. A monument at Peterborough stands to the memory of James Irvine who drowned when attempting to cross Curdies River in 1919.

Right: The Great Ocean Road has opened up not just the communities of Victoria's south west, but the remarkable landscapes and beaches which are regularly enjoyed by visitors from all around the world.

The story of the Great Ocean Road is an old one, beginning at least 20,000 years ago with the Wathaurong, Gadubanud and Girai wurrung people of the Kulin Nation. The Wathaurong lived along the coast between Werribee River and Lorne, with their land stretching inland towards Ballarat. Known as the 'King Parrot' people, the Gadubanud lived amongst the rainforest and coastlines of the Otways, while the Girai wurrung lived between Warrnambool's Hopkins River and Princetown. Of these people most is known of the Wathaurong, who befriended escaped convict William Buckley in 1803, believing him to be 'Murrangurk', a recently deceased warrior who had come back to life. Buckley lived with the Wathaurong for 32 years before entering John Batman's camp at Indented Head to tell his story. As European influence began to spread across the landscape, first with explorers, whalers and sealers, followed by timber cutters, pastoralists, settlers and tourists, small towns and villages were established along the coast and hinterland. In the early days many of these communities were remote, relying on the sea for access and supplies. An increasing population naturally led to more ships travelling along the south west coast, with many coming to grief as they failed to navigate the treacherous waters successfully. The local museums are full of photographs and artefacts putting a human face to the thousands of lives lost. It wasn't until after the turn of the 20th century that many of these communities became easily accessible, thanks to the Great Ocean Road.

ECONOMY

The Great Ocean Road region falls within the local government areas of the Surf Coast, Colac Otway, Corangamite and Warrnambool shires, encompassing an area of just over 11,000 square kilometres and a population of 101,000 people. Covering a diverse area of rural and urban centres, the economic profile can vary dramatically from one locale to another. Key industries for the Surf Coast, Colac Otway and Corangamite shires include manufacturing, agriculture, forestry, fishing, construction and tourism, while for Warrnambool healthcare is also significant. For a region founded in agriculture, it is no surprise that it is one of the leading industries, contributing over $1 billion dollars to the economy.

While tourism isn't strictly an industry in itself, large numbers of visitors to the region have a tremendous impact on industries such as retail, food, transport and accommodation. Known as the 'Visitor Economy', tourism injects over another $1 billon annually into the economy while supporting over 4,000 jobs. Tourism has long been recognised as a significant contributor, and was a decisive factor in the shutting down of logging in the Otways: the two were seen to be incompatible. With icons such as the 12 Apostles and London Bridge gaining world-wide attention and a commitment to provide world class visitor experiences, tourism is only going to grow.

Left: Agriculture is still a way of life for many in the Great Ocean Road region and an important contributor to economic prosperity.

Above: Iconic locations such as the 12 Apostles, London Bridge and Bells Beach draw large crowds throughout the year, helping to drive the 'Visitor Economy' to the benefit of the local communities.

CULTURE

The culture and heritage of the region through which the Great Ocean Road passes is built on a rich tapestry framed within a rugged landscape where shadows of the past intertwine. Long before European explorers and settlers arrived, the Wathaurong, Gadubanud and Girai wurrung people of the Kulin Nation moved with the seasons along the coastline and through the forests of the Otways. Locations such as Bells Beach offered a plentiful food source and was once a place to meet and trade, with middens still to be found along the coastline today. Holding a deep spiritual connection to the land, names such as Mangowak for Painkalac Creek Estuary, meaning 'a good place for hunting swans', were aptly descriptive.

Whalers and sealers had begun to operate along the coastline around 1800, with the Henty Brothers establishing a whaling statin at Apollo Bay in the 1840s. By the mid 1860s pastoral runs were being established, followed by subdivision of land and the establishment of towns. Sadly, as indigenous and European cultures intersected there were points of friction ending in violence, with several known massacres of indigenous groups.

With European settlement gaining in momentum, the number of ships passing the small coastal towns of South West Victoria increased, as did the number of ships wrecked nearby forging a maritime history born of tragedy and courage. The late 1800s also saw the development of early tourism as visitors fell in love with the coastline, often coming to Torquay for a picnic and to fish by Spring Creek. With the opening of the Great Ocean Road in 1932, the towns of South West Victoria were opened up and tourism began to grow. The pioneering of surfing at Bells Beach in the 1930s was a key factor in the birth of Australian beach culture and the surf industry.

Above: Gibson Steps, where cultures intersect. The modern 86 steps offer safe passage down to the beach, enhancing the legacy of Hugh Gibson and earlier the Girai wurrung people who were the first to cut steps into the limestone cliffs, opening access to the shore.

WILDLIFE

From the mighty southern right whales which migrate north out of Antarctic waters each year to the humble glow worms nestled amongst Melba Gully, the Great Ocean Road offers the opportunity for many encounters with the region's wildlife. Dawn and dusk are often the best times to spot wildlife, as many species such as the shy platypus of Lake Elizabeth in the Great Otway National Park are nocturnal. Kennett River and Cape Otway are famous for their large colonies of koalas which rest in manna gums lining the roads, while Anglesea golf course offers the chance to play a round amongst the resident population of eastern grey kangaroos. Koalas, emus, wallabies, kangaroos and waterbirds all thrive in the extinct volcano of Tower Hill, Victoria's oldest national park. Birdlife is plentiful in the wetlands, heathlands and forests with over 150 species to be seen including albatross, mutton birds, hooded plovers, king parrots and birds of prey such as the peregrine falcon and nankeen kestrel. In warmer weather, you may also encounter reptiles such as blue tongue lizards and the occasional brown or tiger snake.

Marine life is plentiful, with dolphins a common site along the coast and a large colony of Australian fur seals on Hayley Reef within the Marengo Marine Sanctuary, just 50 meters offshore. At night, penguins emerge from the surf and waddle up the beach to their rookeries at the 12 Apostles and London Bridge. Watching southern right whales nursing their calves in the Logan's Beach Whale Nursery during the winter months however, is the ultimate of animal encounters for many who travel the Great Ocean Road.

Opposite page: A southern right whale breaches majestically at Marengo near Apollo Bay. Considered endangered, there are approximately 300 residing in the waters off South East Australia.

Above: With its distinctive 3 note, high pitched song, the flame robin can be found in the Otway Ranges. The males of the species have beautiful orange feathers covering their breast and throat.

Left: Brown and tiger snakes may be encountered on warm sunny days.

WARNING

SNAKES

Far left: Wallabies are just one of the many species you will encounter on a visit to Tower Hill Wildlife Reserve, 30 minutes beyond Warrnambool. Like their larger relative the kangaroo, wallabies are marsupials which raise their young joeys within the safety of a pouch. Surrounded by Tower Hill Lake, the reserve's walking tracks usually lead to the discovery of a variety of water birds, kangaroos, emus and wallabies.

Left: The Australian k ing parrot can seen along the Great Ocean Road in places such as Kennett River, Lorne and the Otways. The local Gadubanud people who lived amongst the Otways are known as the 'King Parrot People'.

Opposite page bottom: The nankeen kestrel is a small bird of prey which can often be seen hovering over grasslands in search of their prey. Keep a lookout as you travel the Great Ocean Road as they can be seen in many locations including the 12 Apostles and Cape Otway Lightstation.

Opposite page middle: Weighing only 10 grams and growing to 13 centimetres, the pink robin is a very small bird which can be found in the cool temperate forests of the Otway Ranges. Females are brown in colour, while males have a beautiful pink breast which contrasts against the dark plumage of their head and wings.

Left: As you explore the beaches and rock pools along the Great Ocean Road, you may encounter colourful starfish.

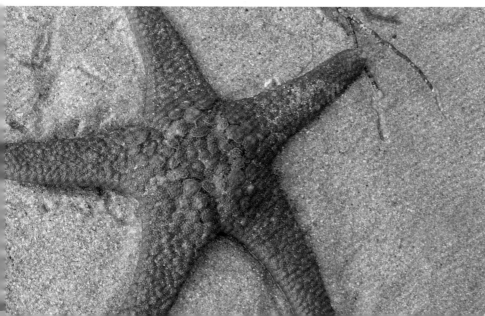

P L A N T L I F E

From windswept coastal heathlands to the remnants of ancient Gondwanan rainforests, there is a surprising variety of plantlife to be found when exploring the Great Ocean Road. Featuring over 700 plant species, which includes over a quarter of Victoria's flora and 80 different types of orchids, Anglesea Heath is richly diverse. Colour erupts in spring as sun and thick lip spider orchids, amongst others, bloom. Along the exposed cliffs of the Port Campbell National Park cushion bush, tussock grass and beard heath thrive in the challenging conditions, while wetlands such as Painkalac Creek Estuary support species including sea rush, creeping brookweed and beaded glasswort. Listed as threatened, remnants of gnarled coastal moonah woodlands can be found around Aireys Inlet, Torquay and Anglesea, helping stabilise the landscape and prevent erosion.

Inland, the forests of the Otway Ranges feel like a landscape that time forgot. Receiving some of the state's highest annual rainfall totals, cool temperate rainforests dominated by myrtle beech and blackwood, intertwined with beautiful fern gullies, thrive. The wet sclerophyll forests of the Otways feature the majestic mountain ash, probably the tallest flowering plant in the world. Logged heavily in the 19th century, few ancient examples survive, with most less than 200 years old.

Far left: Mountain ash (Eucalyptus regnans).

Left: Cushion bush and Carpobrotus glaucescens grow amongst the heathland above Gibson Steps Beach in the Port Campbell National Park.

Bottom right: Koala's love the leaves of manna gums, and in the case of the colony at Cape Otway, possibly a little too much. A large number of trees have been decimated, requiring a revegetation program.

Bottom far left: Ferns are prominent amongst the rainforests of the Otway Ranges. Taking 30 minutes, the Maits Rest Rainforest Walk is a great way to experience the rainforest.

TORQUAY

The sun rises over the ocean swell, its sweet light dancing across the landscape; painting famous beaches and weathered cliffs in shades of red and yellow it greets a new day. Only one and a half hours from Melbourne, yet seemingly a world away, Torquay is where adventure on the Great Ocean Road begins. With its back beach, Jan Juc, and Bells Beach just down the road, Torquay has been blessed by geography and weather patterns which have created the world class breaks from which the Australian surfing industry was born. However, the anchor of the Joseph H Scammell standing on the front beach reminds us that this rugged coastline also has a dark past. The Scammell ran aground on a reef near Point Danger, driven towards the shore in rough seas on 7th May 1891. The crew and passengers survived, while the cargo washed ashore to be looted by locals.

A vibrant seaside resort town, there is a wealth of experiences for the visitor exploring the area. The Surf Coast walk is a major draw for those who love trekking: a wonderfully sensory experience, traversing beaches and windswept bluffs. Vintage aircraft lovers can enjoy Tiger Moth flights from Torquay airport and get a unique perspective of this beautiful area into the bargain.

Above: Just a short walk from the centre of town, Torquay's Back Beach, set against a grassy foreshore complete with BBQs, is a favourite with beginner surfers.

Right: The Australian National Surfing Museum celebrates Australia's surfing history, with displays that include boards used by four-time world champion, Australian surfer Mark Richards.

Previous page: Built to honour the memory of those who fell in World War I by their mates who returned, the Great Ocean Road holds a special place in the hearts of Australians. The famous archway at Eastern View pays tribute to both the fallen and the road builders.

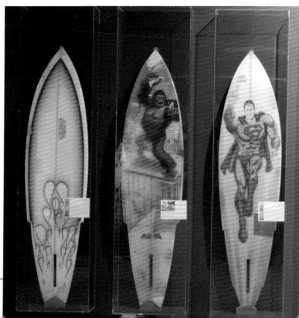

BELLS BEACH

Just a short distance from Torquay lies Australia's spiritual home of surfing, Bells Beach, where Australian surfing really came into its own with the inauguration of the country's longest running surfing competition, the Bells Beach Surf Classic (now the Rip Curl Pro). As you stand atop the weathered limestone cliffs amidst the coastal heathland, spare a thought for the keen locals who originally pioneered surfing at Bells in the late 1930s. In those days there was no easy access to the beach, surfers either came in by sea or endured a scramble down the cliffs from an old Cobb and Co. coach track which ran along the headland. It wasn't until 1960, that a track down to the beach was finally opened.

Declared a 'Surfing Recreation Reserve' in 1971, Bells is listed by the Heritage council of Victoria for its natural, social and historical significance. Once a meeting place for the Wathaurong people who collected crayfish and abalone at low tide, Bells has become an icon on the international stage, drawing the world's best surfers in a migration known as 'The Pilgrimage' to compete in in the annual Rip Curl Pro event.

Left: Winkipop lookout provides stunning views of Bells Beach. It has been observed by some that the towering limestone cliffs create a natural amphitheater, from which to watch the surf and those who take it on.

Below: The best surf at Bells occurs during the autumn and winter months, as strong lows drive swell towards shore. Crossing a shallow reef, the swell slows and shapes to create the famous Rincon and Bells Bowl breaks.

ANGLESEA

Resting amidst bushland on the banks of the Anglesea River, on a coastline whose rugged cliffs soak up the warm hues of the rising sun, Anglesea is where the road first really meets the Ocean. Once known as Swampy Creek, the area was popular with early adventurers who travelled from Melbourne to camp by the river and fish. Today the river remains a popular location for canoeing, fishing and observing the local birdlife. The bathing boxes which sit by the riverbank add a rustic charm from yesteryear.

For the nature lover, Anglesea Heath lies to the north of town. This rich ecosystem of heathlands, woodlands and swamps are believed to host a quarter of Victoria's flora species and over 100 species of native birdlife, including the crimson rosella. During spring the area comes to life as wildflowers bloom and a wave of colour sweeps across the landscape.

A great day here starts with a romantic sunrise and spectacular views across Anglesea from Loveridge Lookout, and can continue with a stroll along part of the Surf Coast Walk on the way to Point Roadknight, a spot of fishing or a swim in the surf on Anglesea's main beach. For those who love a bit of adrenaline, Victoria's first professionally designed mountain cross track awaits at Anglesea bike park.

■ Above: The Wathaurong people who lived in the area for thousands of years knew Anglesea as Kuarka-dorla, indicating the river was a good place to fish for mullet.

Right: Anglesea Golf Club is famous for its resident population of eastern grey kangaroos, which graze along the fairways in the early morning and late afternoon. The club's kangaroo tour runs daily for a close up view or play a round of golf and the kangaroos will watch you from the shadows as they rest during the day.

Below: Roadknight Beach lies to the south of Anglesea's main beach, sheltered from the southerly swell and wind by Point Roadknight, a limestone dune which stretches out from Urquhart Bluff into Bass Strait. A popular swimming location for families when patrolled, rock pools and fascinating weathered rock formations, fashioned as the wind and ocean erode the landscape, wait to be explored.

AIREY'S INLET

As you follow the Great Ocean Road from Anglesea to Lorne, a well-known landmark soon comes into view. Known affectionately as the 'White Queen', Split Point Lighthouse rests high atop the windswept cliffs of Aireys Inlet. This tranquil coastal town sits amongst bushland on the edge of Painkalac Creek Valley and a timeworn coastline of sandy beaches, rock platforms, eroding cliffs and the remnants of a volcanic past.

Flowing from the foothills of the Otway Ranges, Painkalac Creek snakes across the river floodplain dividing Aireys Inlet from Fairhaven, before feeding into a beautiful estuary behind Split Point which breaks out into Bass Strait after heavy rain. Home to an abundance of wildlife, the Wathaurong and Gadubanud people knew the estuary as Mangowak, meaning 'a good place for hunting swans'.

The Surf Coast Walk draws to an end as it traverses the 30 metre-high bluffs of Aireys Inlet and descends to Fairhaven Beach. Offering spectacular views along the coast, it is well worth experiencing the Aireys Clifftops (2.8 kilometre) and Lighthouse Discovery (2.1 kilometre) sections of the walk. At low tide, make your way down to the beach below the lighthouse and explore the rock pools. You may just be lucky enough to see crabs, starfish or an octopus hiding amongst the rocks.

■ Right: As you drive from Aireys Inlet to Fairhaven remember that Australian human history dates back many thousands of years. Long before European settlement, Painkalac Creek created a natural boundary between the Wathaurong people in the east and the Gadubanud people in the west.

Above: With ten shipwrecks occurring along the Surf Coast before 1890, Split Point Lighthouse was built by the Chance Brothers and brought into operation on 1st September 1891. Standing 66 metres above sea level, the lamp of the White Queen watches out to sea, keeping passing ships safe on this rugged coast today, just as it did over a century ago.

Below: Standing 20 metres high, Eagle Rock is an ancient volcanic stack with a limestone cap which formed as marine sediment slowly accumulated and then eroded. Along with Table Rock, these formations create a haven for marine life and are protected within the 17 hectare Eagle Rock Marine Sanctuary. A number of fish species inhabit the sanctuary including blue-throated wrasse and the yellow-striped leatherjacket.

ORNE

■ Above: Lorne Pier stretches 196 metres out into Louttit Bay. With a large platform at the end, it is the most popular location to drop a line into the bay. It is also the start of Lorne's famous Pier to Pub 1.2-kilometre swim.

On a sunny day as the azure water and white sand of Louttit Bay contrast against the lush greens of the rolling hinterland, it is easy to see why this gorgeous seaside village has enchanted visitors for over a century. Author Rudyard Kipling was so moved by a visit to Lorne in 1891, he wrote the poem Flowers with the lines "Gathered where the Erskine leaps; down the road to Lorne".

Lorne's picturesque coastline is a series of rock shelves, with a gorgeous sandy main beach, which begins at the mouth of the Erskine River and runs 1.2 kilometres south to the edge of Point Grey. Recognised as one of Victoria's most popular beaches, Lorne's main beach is patrolled on the southern end and is a great location for those trying their hand at surfing for the first time.

Stepping away from the coast and lacing up your walking boots, there are a remarkable 10 significant waterfalls, nestled amongst the hinterland, within 10 kilometres of Lorne, just waiting to delight your senses. Just a 15-minute drive from Lorne, Erskine Falls is the most popular with visitors. Parking at the head of the Erskine Falls Road, the 300 metres of stairs to the first viewing platform are well worth the effort. Visitors can soak up the scent of moist rainforest air and listen to the burble of the Erskine River as it tumbles 30 metres into the gully below.

Above: A visit to Lorne would be incomplete without a walk across the town's famous swing bridge, spanning the Erskine River. Built in 1934, the bridge is an iconic stop along the Great Ocean Road.

Right: More experienced walkers can take the 15-kilometre return walk along the Erskine River from Lorne to the base of the falls.

Previous page: Located on the southern side of Lorne, with easy access from the car park on George Street, Teddy's Lookout is a must as you pass through the area. Soak up the sweeping views along the coastline as you watch the Great Ocean Road snake into the distance, hugging the ocean cliffs.

Wye River and Kennett River lie on a spectacular stretch of the Great Ocean Road between Lorne and Apollo Bay. Here you hug the cliffs backing onto the Great Otway National Park, with views towards a coastline of rock ledges and sandy beaches. It was first settled in 1882 when brothers Alex and Donald McRae, along with their cousin Alex McLennan, arrived in search of land for farming. The McRae brothers settled at Wye River, while Alex McLennan settled 5 kilometres further along the coast at Kennett River.

Nestled between the foothills of the Great Otway National Park, both Wye River and Kennett River offer a spectacular backdrop to their beautiful beaches, where the rivers which bear their names empty into Bass Strait. Popular for swimming and surfing, both beaches are patrolled during peak holiday seasons and with rescues occurring each year, it is wise to swim between the flags. For those who love to fish, the river estuaries, rock ledges and beaches along this coast are very popular.

A 90-minute heritage walk, which starts at the foreshore and finishes at Separation creek, explores the history of Wye River. A touch of maritime history lies a few kilometres to the north, with the wreck of the W.B. Godfrey visible at low tide near the 'Lonely Grave'. If you are seeking a nighttime adventure, take a walk amongst the glow worms of Grey River Reserve.

Above: Wye River flows down from the Otway Ranges through the town of Wye River, creating an estuary a kilometre long which supports a variety of fish life including the Australian Grayling and Tasmanian Mudfish.

KENNETT RIVER

Above: Kennett River forms at the confluence of its east and west branches within the Otway Ranges, flowing 10 kilometres before reaching Bass Strait. As you explore the area keep an eye out for king parrots, fairy wrens, kookaburras and cockatoos.

Right: Everybody loves a koala and Kennett River's famous Koala Walk amongst the manna gums on Grey River Road is a great place to see them.

APOLLO BAY

Originally named Krambruk meaning 'sandy place', Apollo Bay is an idyllic coastal village nestled between rolling hills and the shoreline of a 3-kilometre long sweeping bay. Protected by Point Bunbury and harbour's breakwater, the southern end of the bay is sheltered and perfect for swimming when the beach is patrolled. To the north and away from the harbour, waves grow in size offering opportunities for surfing, with the best conditions in autumn and winter.

Resting in the foothills of the Otways, Apollo Bay is a nature lover's paradise where the coast meets the rainforest. Watch southern right and humpback whales migrate from Antarctica in autumn and back again in spring, walk along sandy beaches, explore rock pools or head into the ranges and walk amongst ancient rainforest as you discover glow worms and explore spectacular waterfalls. For the fit and prepared, the Great Ocean Road Walk will allow you to experience the rugged coast first hand as you track 35-kilometre from Apollo Bay to Princetown, finishing near the 12 Apostles.

Above: The harbour is one of the Apollo Bay's most distinctive features. Enclosed by two breakwaters, it is home to the local fishing fleet and an important asset to the local economy. Providing sweeping views of the bay, the breakwaters make for a relaxing short walk and an opportunity to catch dinner.

Left: On a clear night when conditions are right, the Aurora Australis can be seen along the Great Ocean Road from Apollo Bay.

THE OTWAYS

Left: The 3-kilometre walk amongst mountain ash, myrtle beach and ferns to Beauchamp Falls is rewarding, but strenuous. Be sure to allow yourself plenty of time to complete the walk comfortably.

Right: Planted in the 1930s, the Californian Redwoods near Beach Forest are a spectacular sight. Around 60 metres tall, daylight struggles through the canopy, creating a setting akin to that of a forest within a fairytale.

Below: Facing the Southern Ocean and framed by 30-100 metre-high dunes, Johanna Beach is breathtakingly beautiful and is one of the most popular locations to camp along the Great Ocean Road.

Previous page: Hopetoun Falls is resplendent amongst a lush cover of ferns. Fed by the Aire River, as it tumbles over a sheer drop and crashes into the rocks below, the sound of rushing water fills the valley.

The Great Otway National Park and Otway Forest Park protect an area of over 103,000 hectares, from Anglesea in the east to Princetown in the west and then inland towards Colac. Declared in 2006, the Otway Forest Park incorporates forests on the northern side of the Otway Ranges, while the Great Otway National Park, declared in 2004, encompasses a diverse and stunning landscape of waterfalls secluded within ancient rainforest, towering mountain ash, windswept heathlands and historic coastline.

Recently expanded to include the Anglesea Heath, the Great Otway National Park is where forest and sea meet, providing spectacular backdrops to the towns of Lorne, Wye River and Kennett River. Along the 100-kilometre 'Great Ocean Walk', stretching from Apollo Bay to Princetown, numerous entry and exit points create opportunities for day walkers to experience the Great Otway National Park in a personal way. Opportunities include discovering the lonely solitude of Moonlight Head's Wreck Beach or camping under the stars at Johanna Beach, named after the schooner 'Johanna' which was wrecked nearby in 1843.

Away from the coast and amongst the cool temperate rainforest of the Otways, a walk amongst ancient mountain ash, rewards the visitor with lungfuls of fresh moist air and the burbling sound of water resonating in the distance. Here you will find an abundance of waterfalls, including the spectacular Hopetoun Falls, Triplet Falls and Beauchamp Falls, each with their own charm. A walk amongst the ancient myrtle forest of Melba Gully (an area with one of the highest rainfalls within Victoria) will reveal the magic of glow worms at night.

CAPE OTWAY

Much of Cape Otway falls within the Great Otway National Park, which makes for a relaxing scenic drive as the road slowly leads you down to the most southerly point of Victoria.

Home to the oldest surviving lighthouse on mainland Australia, the Cape Otway coast is rugged and unforgiving. Here the Southern Ocean meets Bass Strait on a coastline where at least 8 ships have been lost to the sea. Coming into service in 1848, the lighthouse became known as the 'Beacon of Hope', providing safe passage to ships as they 'threaded the needle' between Cape Otway and King Island in preparation for entering Port Phillip Heads.

The facilities at the lighthouse grew over time to include a telegraph station in 1859 after a submarine cable was laid between Victoria and Tasmania. Operating until 1902, the Royal Australian Navy recommissioned the Telegraph Station during World War II, and operated alongside the US radar station which was established after the SS City of Rayville was sunk by a German mine off the coast.

There is much to explore at Cape Otway, so allow plenty of time. On a clear day during winter and spring months, you may be lucky enough to spot migrating whales as they come close to shore during their migration.

Above: After months at sea, Cape Otway was a welcome sight, indicating a ship had successfully navigated the treacherous Shipwreck Coast with their journey nearing its end.

Left: The Cape Otway lighthouse is a tangible link to Victoria's seafaring past. It is possible to spend a night in the old keeper's cottages and experience a touch of what life may have been like on this windswept coast back in the 1800s.

Following page: At low tide the anchor of the Marie Gabrielle emerges from the sea on the aptly named Wreck Beach, a haunting symbol of the many ships and lives claimed by the Shipwreck Coast.

Setting sale from Gravesend, England on the 1st of March 1878, under Captain George Gibb, the Loch Ard carried 52 crew and passengers, including Doctor Evory Carmichael, his wife Rebecca and 6 children. Only days from making landfall in Melbourne, the Loch Ard encountered overcast skies, preventing Captain Gibb from taking readings to establish the ship's position ahead of a safe passage between Cape Otway and King Island. Concerned, Captain Gibb stayed on deck the night of May 31st with a watch looking out for the Cape Otway lighthouse. The sea had been rough and the night dark as the Loch Ard sailed through a heavy mist. At 5am on June 1st breakers were heard, and the mist lifted suddenly revealing towering limestone cliffs immediately ahead. Taking evasive action, the captain attempted to sail away from the coast, then dropped the anchors in a last desperate effort to avoid disaster. Sadly, all was in vain and as the Loch Ard struck the reef at the base of Mutton Bird Island the ship's fate was sealed.

As the tragedy unfolded, of the many washed into the sea, apprentice Tom Pearce and Eva Carmichael managed to avoid drowning. Tom was the first to reach the shore, having spent time drifting while clinging to a capsized lifeboat. Eva eventually drifted into the gorge clinging to debris from the wreck. Hearing her calls for help, Tom reentered the freezing water and helped her to dry land. Once safely ashore, Tom found shelter for Eva in a nearby cave before scaling the treacherous cliffs to raise the alarm and return with help. As the Loch Ard slipped beneath the waves, Tom and Eva entered history as the only two survivors of the Shipwreck Coast's greatest tragedy.

Far left: The Loch Ard was a 3-masted clipper ship, operated by the Loch Line of Glasgow.

Top: Tom Pearce the ship's apprentice and Eva Carmichael, an 18 year-old Irish immigrant, were the sole survivors of the Loch Ard disaster. Although the public hoped Tom and Eva would marry, they parted ways with Tom returning to the sea and Eva to Ireland.

Left: Whatever remains of the Loch Ard lies at the base of Mutton Bird Island, near Loch Ard Gorge.

PORT CAMPBELL NATIONAL

Previous page: In an ever-changing coastline, the 12 Apostles are a temporary beauty. In time, they will return to the ocean from whence they came.

Above: Gog and Magog bask in the glow of the rising sun on a calm morning on Gibson Beach.

Right: London Bridge collapsed on 15th January 1990, leaving two people stranded; they were later rescued by helicopter.

PARK

Hauntingly beautiful, the sea stacks and islands of the Port Campbell National Park stand out in the Southern Ocean on a wave sculpted coastline of arches, gorges, bays and blowholes hewn from golden yellow limestone. First captivating tourists in the late 1880s, and amongst the most dramatic coastlines in Australia, Port Campbell National Park was declared on 5th May 1964 with 700 hectares set aside for protection. Today the national park covers an area from Point Ronald at Princetown to Curdies Inlet at Peterborough, taking in 1750 hectares, including delicate coastal heathlands which bloom with wildflower colours in spring. Famous for the 12 Apostles and London Bridge, there is so much more to be seen and experienced within the national park that it is wise to spend a few days exploring all it has to offer. Discover the scale of the landscape as you walk along Gibson Beach in the shadow of Gog and Magog at the base of the 70 metre-high cliffs. Explore Loch Ard Gorge and marvel at how shipwreck survivor Tom Pearce managed to scale the towering cliffs. Listen to the ocean surge into Thunder Cave and discover the formations of the Razorback, Grotto and Arch. For memories to last a lifetime, rug the family up and venture out at dusk to London Bridge and the 12 Apostles and witness the penguins returning to shore after fishing at sea. Remember, this coastline is unstable and always keep to designated walking tracks.

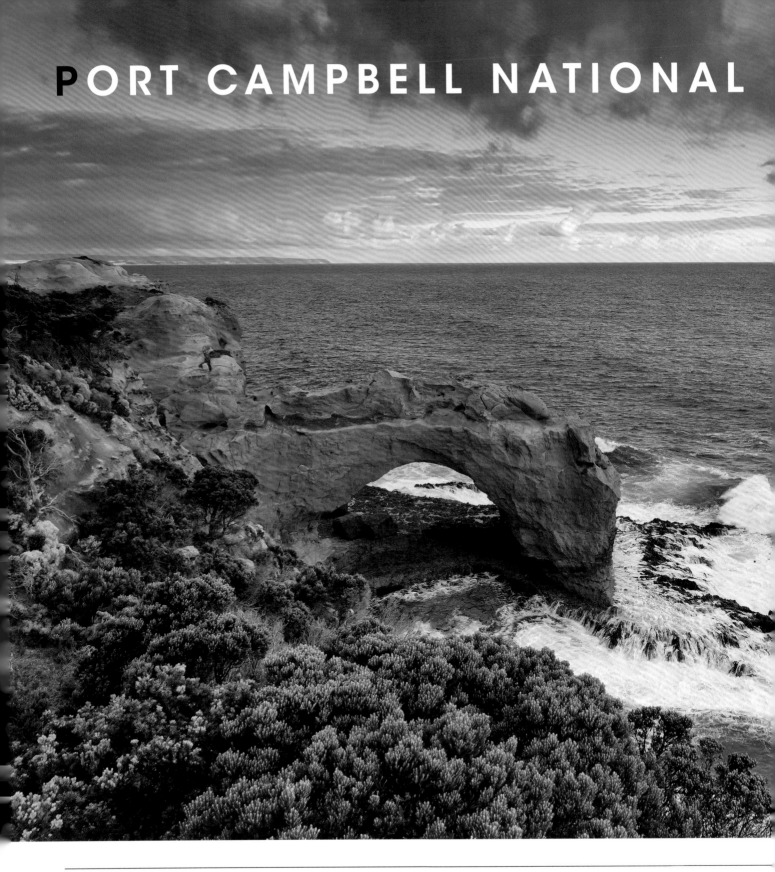

PORT CAMPBELL NATIONAL

PARK

Left: The Arch, which lies just beyond Port Campbell, is one of the less visited yet still spectacular formations of the national park. It is remarkable the beauty that time and the elements can etch into the landscape.

Below: Tom Pearce and Eva Carmichael washed into Loch Ard Gorge after their ship struck Mutton Bird Island on 1st June 1878. Tom managed to scale the cliffs and raise the alarm while Eva sheltered in a cave behind the beach.

Bottom: When you visit Loch Ard Gorge and take the clifftop walk, be sure to visit the Razorback. Long, narrow and tall it impressively lives up to its name.

PORT CAMPBELL

Framed within a picturesque limestone gorge and largely protected from the wrath of the Southern Ocean, Port Campbell is the only shelter for vessels between Apollo Bay and Warrnambool. Settled in the 1870s, Port Campbell was named after Captain Alexander Campbell, the manager of the whaling station at Port Fairy who was known to shelter in the bay as he sailed between Port Fairy and King Island.

Today, just a 10-minute drive from the 12 Apostles and 7 minutes from London Bridge, Port Campbell is a popular base from which to explore some of the Great Ocean Road's most beloved icons. There is, however, much more to Port Campbell than meets the eye and for those who love to experience local produce, the 75-kilometre 12 Apostle Gourmet Trail mixes beautiful scenery with chocolate, cheese, ice cream, nuts and beer.

Be sure to explore Port Campbell's maritime heritage by stopping into the visitor information centre which hosts an extensive collection of relics from the Loch Ard, Newfield, Falls of Halladale, Fiji and Schomberg shipwrecks. The Rocket Shed on the eastern side of the bay, built after the Loch Ard tragedy, allowed a crew to fire lines out to foundering ships, hauling their passengers and crew to safety.

An area with a rich indigenous culture, middens along the coastline are a tangible reminder of the Girai wurrung people who lived here not so long ago. Being one with the land, they knew the headland as Purroitchihoorrong, 'the spirit voice that mocks you'. If you explore the clifftops on the Port Campbell Discovery walk, and listen to the Southern Ocean churning against the cavernous coastline, perhaps you will hear the spirit mocking you too.

Left: On a treacherous coastline, with very few locations which could be considered safe for swimming, Port Campbell's bay is blessed with a beautiful sandy beach, patrolled by the Port Campbell Surf Lifesaving Club. The foreshore has picnic tables and a boat ramp at the Campbell's Creek end of the beach. Although usually calm, rips can form off the beach when there is a heavy swell on the bay.

Above: Port Campbell's professional cray fishing fleet launch their boats from the jetty by crane. Set in deep water, it is a popular recreational fishing location. Throwing a line in is a relaxing way to pause and listen to the Southern Ocean lapping against the pylons beneath your feet.

BAY OF ISLANDS COASTAL

PARK

Left: On a sunny day the yellow of the limestone coastline contrasts beautifully against the azure blue of the bay, while the coastal heathlands erupt in colour as wildflowers bloom in spring.

Right: Sailing in heavy fog on 14th November 1908, the Falls of Halladale ran aground at Halladale Point, near Peterborough.

Sixteen kilometres to the west of Port Campbell, well away from the crowds of the 12 Apostles, lies Peterborough and the picturesque Bay of Islands Coastal Park. Starting near the Peterborough golf course, the coastal park stretches 32 kilometres towards Warrnambool and, like so much of the Shipwreck Coast, the names of bays, beaches and reefs tell a story woven around the many ships which came to grief.

A highlight of the coastal park is the remarkable Bay of Islands and Bay of Martyrs, with each offering breathtaking views from clifftop platforms. Here limestone stacks, weathered remnants of an ancient, receding coastline, stand resolute against time and the churn of the Southern Ocean which will nonetheless eventually reclaim them. The clifftop walk, from the Bay of Martyrs back towards Wild Dog Cove, taking in Halladale Point, never fails to stimulate the senses.

Amongst the beauty however, there are two names which contrast starkly with the picture-perfect landscape: the Bay of Martyrs and Massacre Bay. According to legend a group of local Aboriginal people were murdered nearby in the early days of European settlement.

WARRNAMBOOL

Having led you on an exploration of windswept beaches, ancient rainforests and tales of shipwrecks, the Great Ocean Road draws to its conclusion at Allansford on the outskirts of Warrnambool. Set between farmland and the Southern Ocean on the banks of the Merri and Hopkins Rivers, Warrnambool is believed to have taken its name from the nearby volcanic cone of Mount Warrnambool which to the local Gunditjmara people fittingly means "land between two rivers". Although History tells us the first European visit to the area was the voyage of Lieutenant James Grant in the Lady Nelson as she sailed along the coastline in December 1800, the legend of the "Mahogany Ship" suggests Cristóvão de Mendonça may have explored the coastline on behalf of the Portuguese in 1521-1524. With a strong maritime history, it is fitting that Warrnambool is home to the Flagstaff Hill Maritime Museum, where tales of tragic shipwrecks come to life as you explore relics retrieved from the ocean. Here visitors learn about the Loch Ard and marvel at the Minton porcelain peacock which survived the famous disaster.

The 3-kilometre Heritage Trail is a great introduction, taking in some of Warrnambool's buildings of yesteryear including the old Court House. Another worthwhile walk (or cycle) is the 5.7-kilometre Foreshore Promenade from the Breakwater, around Lady Bay and on to Logan's Beach whale nursery. Walkers will also often want to explore the Thunder Point Coastal Reserve, its wetlands and weatherworn coast. If you have seen the movie Oddball, be sure to take a tour of Middle Island to meet the maremma dogs who protect the resident penguin colony.

Left: At Flagstaff Hill history lifts off the pages of books and the tales of shipwrecks and lives lost along the Shipwreck Coast come to life. Learn about the newly married Captain Gibb, whose last words to Loch Ard survivor Eva Carmichael were "If you are saved Eva, let my dear wife know that I died like a sailor".

Below: Lake Pertobe can be found just behind the Foreshore Promenade of Warrnambool's Lady Bay. Featuring walking paths, an adventure playground, boats and BBQ facilities, the precinct is perfect for families.

Bottom: Each year between May and October migrating southern right whales return to the protected waters of Lady Bay. These majestic creatures can be seen from the viewing platforms of Logan's Beach as they breach or slap the water with their tails.

ACKNOWLEDGEMENTS

The author would like to thank all the gifted photographers whose work is featured here. He would particularly like to thank Cristina Baccino and Chris Farrell, both of whom have been generous with their knowledge and time. Chris would also like to thank Andrew Swaffer for his patience, guidance and commissioning the series; Cristine Schiedel who has beautifully laid out this book; and Jenny Cowan for the map. Thanks to the Australian National Surfing Museum in Torquay for their image and assistance. Love always to Mum, Margaret Munn.

ABOUT THE AUTHOR

Chris Munn is the co-author, with Craig Lewis, of Alpine Australia - A Celebration of the Australian Alps. His earliest memories of the Great Ocean Road are as a child on family holidays to Wye River with his parents and grandparents. Based in Yackandanda at the foothills of the Victorian High Country, Chris spends much of his time exploring and photographing Falls Creek, Mount Hotham and Mount Buffalo. When away from the camera, Chris is an avid runner who competes in 10-kilometre and half marathon events.

ABOUT THE PUBLISHERS

The Australian Geographic journal is a geographical magazine founded in 1986. It mainly covers stories about Australia - its geography, culture, wildlife and people - and six editions are published every year. Australian Geographic also publish a number of books every year on similar subjects for both children and adults. A portion of the profits goes to the Australian Geographic Society which supports scientific research as well as environmental conservation, community projects and Australian adventurers. www.australiangeographic.com.au.

Woodslane Press are a book publishing company based in Sydney, Australia. They are the publishers of Australia's best-selling walking guides and under their co-owned Boiling Billy imprint also publish camping, bush exploration and 4WD guides. For more than a decade committed to publishing books that empower Australians to better explore and understand their own country, Woodslane Press is proud to be working with Australian Geographic to produce this new series of souvenir books. www.woodslane.com.au.

Also available:

PICTURE CREDITS

Front Cover Image : CnOra/iStock (12 Apostles)
Rear Cover Image : canbalci/iStock (Great Ocean Road Street Sign)

pi: Cristina Baccino (Cockatoo, Kennett River)
pii: Chris Munn (Koala, Cape Otway)
p1: MichelleMealing/iStock(Split Point Lighthouse)
p2: ymgerman/iStock (Great Ocean Road Lorne)
p4-5: Chris Farrell Nature Photography (Prince town Wetlands); Micaela del Barro (Bush walker on Wreck Beach)
p6-7: tsvibrav/iStock (Main); tsvibrav/iStock (Tower Hill Reserve Crater Lake)
p8-9: Chris Munn
p10-11: wallix/iStock (Main); Ikonya/iStock (Lorne)
p12-13: Zoya_Avenirovna/iStock (Main); jax10289/ iStock (12 Apostles)
p14: sasimoto/iStock
p16-17: Chris Farrell Nature Photography (Southern Right Whale); Cristina Baccino (Male Flame Robin); jax10289/iStock (Snake Warning)
p18-19: florencemcginn/iStock (Wallaby); Chris Farrell Nature Photography (Nankeen Kestrel); Cristina Baccino (Male Pink Robin & King Parrot); primus95/iStock (Starfish)

p20-21: David Bristow/Australian Geographic (Mountain Ash); Ladiras/iStock (Maits Rest); fotofritz16/iStock (Gibson Beach); Owsigor/iStock (Manna Gum)
p22: jax10289/iStock
p24:25: restlesskath/iStock (Main); Image courtesy the Australian National Surfing Museum, Torquay (Surfboards)
p26-27: FiledImage/iStock (Main); ribeiroantonio/ iStock (Surfers)
p28-29: Mike Leonard/Australian Geographic (Main & Kangaroo); Andrew Haysom/iStock (Rock pools)
p30-31: Chris Farrell Nature Photography (Main); Chris Munn (Lighthouse & Eagle Rock)
p32: bennymarty/iStock
p34-35: Amy Feeney/iStock (Main); Namkhang_Chaiphut/iStock (Swing Bridge); BerndC/iStock (Erskine Falls)
p36-37: Chris Farrell Nature Photography (Wye River & Kennett River); Nicole Patience/iStock (Koala)
p38-39: Zetter/iStock (Main); James Russell/iStock (Aurora Australis)
p40: Chris Munn
p42-43: Cristina Baccino(Beauchamp Falls);

PetroGraphy (Johanna Beach); David Bristow/ Australian Geographic (Californian Redwoods)
p44-45: Chris Farrell Nature Photography (Main); Mike Leonard/Australian Geographic (Lighthouse)
p46: sara_winter
p48: Allan C. Green/State Library of Victoria (Loch Ard); unknown/State Library of Victoria (Eva Carmichael/Tom Pearce); Mike Leonard/Australian Geographic (Mutton Bird Island)
p50: Chris Munn
p52: Chris Munn (Main); Mike Leonard/ Australian Geographic (London Bridge)
p54-55: zetter /iStock (Main); Aneurysm/iStock (Loch Ard Gorge); tsvibrav/iStock (Razorback)
p56-57: Chris Munn (Port Campbell Beach & Jetty)
p58-59: fotofritz16/iStock (Main); Allan C. Green/ State Library of Victoria (Falls of Halladale)
p60-61: Zoya_Avenirovna/iStock (Main); Wirepec/ iStock (Lake Pertobe); Michael Garner/ iStock (Logans Beach)